SOUTHWEST BRANCH
ROCK ISLAND PUBLIC LIBRARY
9010 Ridgewood Road
Rock Island, IL 61201

J 796.323 K

Knapp, Ron.

Top 10 basketball scorers

D0734637

DATE DUE

NOV 2 8	JUN 1 7 2003	
FEB 0 9		JAN 1 9 2004
JUL 5		
JUL 21		
NOV 2 0 1997		
OCT 2 6 1998		
MAR 2 2 1999		
JUL 0 6		
APR 1 9 2002		
MAY 1 3 2002		
APR 2 4 2003		
MAY 0 5 2003		

HIGHSMITH #45115

TOP 10 BASKETBALL SCORERS

Ron Knapp

SPORTS TOP 10

ENSLOW PUBLISHERS, INC.

Bloy St. & Ramsey Ave.   P.O. Box 38

Box 777   Aldershot

Hillside, N.J. 07205   Hants GU12 6BP

U.S.A.   U.K.

Copyright © 1994 by Ron Knapp.

All rights reserved.

No part of this book may be reproduced by any means
without the written permission of the publisher.

Library of Congress Cataloging-in-Publication Data

Knapp, Ron.
    Top 10 basketball scorers / by Ron Knapp.
       p. cm.—(Sports top 10)
    Includes bibliographical references (p.) and index.
    ISBN 0-89490-516-3
      1. Basketball players—United States—Biography—Juvenile
literature. [1. Basketball players.] I. Title. II. Title: Top
10 basketball scorers. III. Series.
GV884.A1K635   1994
793.323'092'2—dc20
   [B]   94-15809
                                    CIP
                                    AC

Printed in the United States of America

10 9 8 7 6 5 4 3 2 1

Photo Credits: AP/Wide World Photos, pp. 27, 41; Focus on Sports, pp. 7, 10, 13, 21, 22, 35, 37, 39; Kansas Jayhawks, p. 19; Los Angeles Lakers, p. 9; Mitchell Layton Photography, pp. 14, 17, 30, 33, 42, 45; Philadelphia 76ers, p. 25; Amy E. Powers, p. 29.

Cover Photo: Mitchell Layton Photography.

Interior Design: Richard Stalzer.

CONTENTS

Introduction

EVERY KID ON EVERY PLAYGROUND knows why basketball has become America's most popular sport. It's exciting to watch superstars put the ball through the hoop, and it's fun to do it yourself.

That's why the playgrounds and driveway courts fill up as soon as the games flicker off the TV. All of us want to try the moves we've just seen our heroes use. How many young people have bitten their tongues trying to imitate Michael Jordan?

What's the most exciting basket? A last-second sky hook by Kareem Abdul-Jabbar or a graceful flying dunk by Julius Erving? How about a vicious drive by Karl Malone? Or a clutch sixty-footer by Jerry West?

Read this book. Imitate the shots of these great players. Invent a few of your own. Maybe in a few years other kids will be reading about you and imitating your shots.

CAREER STATISTICS

Player	NBA Seasons	Games	FG%	Rebounds	Blocks*	Steals*	Points	Average
KAREEM ABDUL-JABBAR	20	1,560	.559	17,440	3,189	1,160	38,387	24.6
ELGIN BAYLOR	14	846	.431	11,463	—	—	23,149	27.4
LARRY BIRD	13	897	.496	8,974	755	1,556	21,791	24.3
WILT CHAMBERLAIN	14	1,045	.540	23,924	—	—	31,419	30.1
JULIUS ERVING	11	836	.507	5,601	1,293	1,508	18,364	22.0
MICHAEL JORDAN	9	667	.516	4,219	684	1,815	21,541	32.3
KARL MALONE	9	734	.525	8,058	615	1,037	19,050	26.0
OSCAR ROBERTSON	14	1,040	.485	7,804	—	—	26,710	25.7
JERRY WEST	14	932	.474	5,376	—	—	25,192	27.0
DOMINIQUE WILKINS	12	907	.467	6,295	596	1,274	24,019	26.5

*Statistics for blocked shots and steals were not kept by the NBA until the 1973-1974 season.

KAREEM ABDUL-JABBAR

THE BOSTON CELTICS NEEDED JUST one more victory to clinch the 1974 NBA championship. But they had to take it from Kareem Abdul-Jabbar, Oscar Robertson, and the Milwaukee Bucks.

John Havlicek dropped in a long arching shot to put the Celtics up 101–100 with just seven seconds left. Then Kareem got the ball. He dribbled up to the baseline and looked for an open man. But the Boston defense was airtight. He put up a seventeen-foot hook shot. Nothing but net! The Bucks won, 102–101. That night he was still so excited he couldn't sleep.

Nobody did hook shots like Kareem. The fans called them "sky hooks." Since he was seven feet two inches tall, he would release the ball almost at the same height as the basket. "Nobody could stop the sky hook," said Celtic superstar Larry Bird. "There was nothing you could do except hope that he missed it."[1]

Abdul-Jabbar's basketball career had begun when he was a six-foot five-inch seventh-grader named Lew Alcindor at St. Jude's Elementary School in New York City. A few years later, the tall skinny kid with the Afro led Power Memorial High School to seventy-one straight victories.

At the University of California at Los Angeles, he and the others on the freshmen team beat the UCLA varsity, the NCAA champs, 75–60. By the time he joined the varsity in his sophomore year, the Bruins were unstoppable. They won three straight NCAA titles.

Once he joined the Bucks, he began dominating his NBA opponents. (It was also at this time, after his conversion to

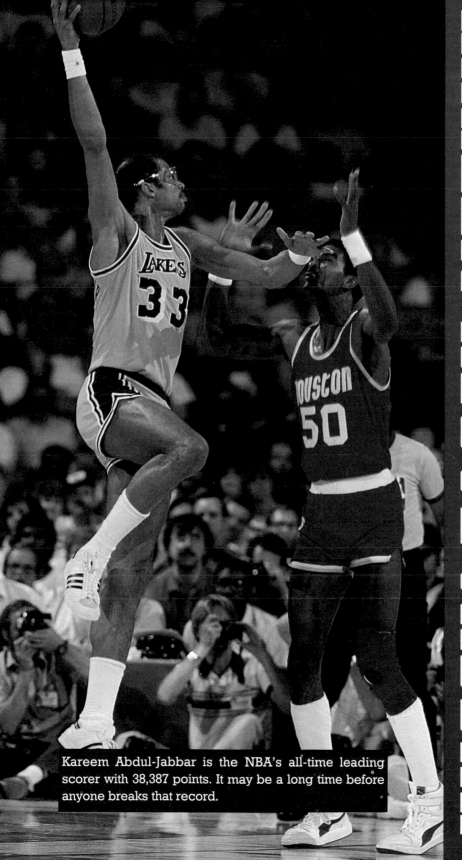

Kareem Abdul-Jabbar is the NBA's all-time leading scorer with 38,387 points. It may be a long time before anyone breaks that record.

KAREEM ABDUL-JABBAR

the Islamic religion, that he changed his name.) Six times during his career he was named league MVP. After five years with Milwaukee, he was traded to the Los Angeles Lakers in 1975. He played fourteen seasons there. At the end of his NBA career, he had 38,387 points, an NBA record.

Early in his career with Milwaukee, Kareem signed an autograph in Detroit for a twelve-year-old fan named Earvin Johnson, Jr. Eight years later, Earvin would be better known as "Magic" and the two men would be teammates on the Lakers of the 1980s, one of the most exciting and successful teams in NBA history. "He was a walking miracle," said Johnson. "Nobody has played at the level Kareem did for so long."[2]

By 1987, the forty-year-old Abdul-Jabbar was playing with goggles, to protect his eyes. He had so little hair left he decided to shave the rest of it off. But in the deciding game of the NBA finals with the Celtics, he ended up with 32 points and four blocked shots. That was the fourth of five championships he and Magic would win with the Lakers.

In the 1960s, fans argued whether Wilt Chamberlain or Bill Russell was the best basketball player of all time. Chamberlain was the greatest scorer, but nobody ever played defense or won championships like Russell. When Kareem became an NBA superstar in the 1970s, fans began comparing him to those two giants. "I think Abdul-Jabbar pretty much combines what Russell and Chamberlain have individually specialized in," said Bob Cousy, then the coach of the Cincinnati Royals.[3] Russell himself had no trouble deciding who was the best. In 1972, he said, "Kareem Abdul-Jabbar is the greatest player to play this game."[4] Over the next seventeen years, Kareem did nothing to change his mind.

KAREEM ABDUL-JABBAR

BORN: April 16, 1947, New York, N.Y.

HIGH SCHOOL: Power Memorial, New York, N.Y.

COLLEGE: UCLA (University of California, Los Angeles)

PRO: Milwaukee Bucks, 1969–1975; Los Angeles Lakers, 1975–1989.

RECORDS: Most seasons played, 20; most points, 38,387; most defensive rebounds in a season, 1,111.

HONORS: NBA MVP, 1971, 1972, 1974, 1976, 1977, 1980; NBA Rookie of the Year, 1970.

Abdul-Jabbar played for an amazing twenty seasons in the NBA and was a member of six championships teams: Milwaukee in 1971 and Los Angeles in 1980, 1982, 1985, 1987, and 1988.

ELGIN BAYLOR

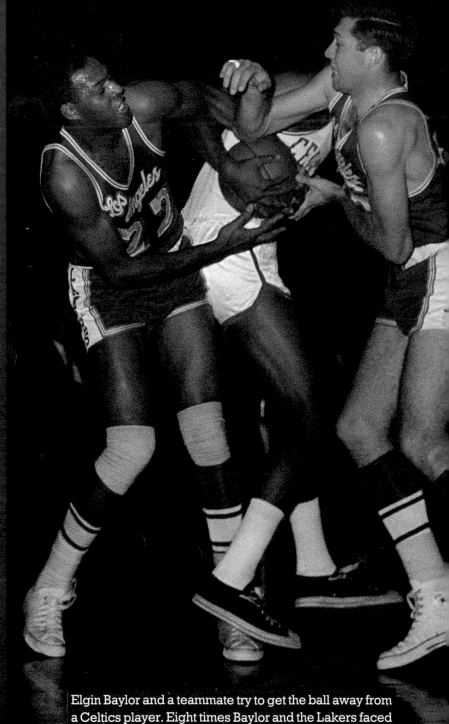

Elgin Baylor and a teammate try to get the ball away from a Celtics player. Eight times Baylor and the Lakers faced the mighty Boston Celtics in the NBA finals, and eight times they were defeated.

ELGIN BAYLOR

HOW DO YOU STOP A man who can fly? In the 1962 NBA finals, the Boston Celtics tried to double-team Elgin Baylor. But that didn't work because he was too good a passer. If Baylor was guarded by two men, he just flipped the ball to an open teammate. In game five, he led the Los Angeles Lakers to a 126–121 victory, with 61 points and 22 rebounds. "Elgin was just a machine," said Satch Sanders, the man who was supposed to guard him.[1]

Baylor was the man who invented "hang time." He seemed to be able to stay up in the air longer than anybody else. Emmett Watson, a reporter, said, "He has never really broken the law of gravity, but he is awfully slow about obeying it."[2]

Elgin was an All-American forward at the University of Seattle. In the 1958 NCAA final, he got 25 points and 19 rebounds, but Kentucky won, 84–72. Then, in his first season with the Minneapolis Lakers, he won Rookie of the Year honors and led them to the NBA finals.

When Baylor was hot nobody could stop him. He scored 55 points in one game during his rookie season. The next year he broke the NBA record with 64. Then he got 71 against the New York Knicks. Nobody except Wilt Chamberlain and David Thompson has ever done better.

In the early 1960s, African-American players in the NBA weren't always treated fairly. Elgin Baylor was one of the first to publicly protest. When he wasn't allowed to stay with the rest of the Lakers in a West Virginia hotel, he refused to play the next game. "I'm a human being," he said. "I'm not an animal put in a cage and let out for the show."[3]

For the 1960–1961 season, the Lakers moved from Minneapolis to Los Angeles and drafted another superstar, Jerry West. The team then had two great scorers. Baylor's acrobatic shots dominated the action under the boards while West ran the offense and dropped in shots from the outside.

In 1965 during a playoff game with the Baltimore Bullets, Elgin fell to the court and severely injured one kneecap. The damage was so extensive that doctors wondered if he'd ever be able to walk again. But he trained hard and was able to rejoin the team the following season. When he returned, though, his flashy, daring moves were a thing of the past. His knee was no longer strong enough for them.

Of course, there had always been more to Elgin's game than just his great moves under the basket. He was still one of the best passers in the league, and he could throw a head fake better than anybody. Nobody ever seemed to know what he was going to do with the ball. Richie Guerin, of the New York Knicks, said it was impossible to stay with him: "He's either got three hands or two basketballs. It's like guarding a flood."[4]

By the time Baylor retired in 1971, he was the third-highest scorer in NBA history. Only Michael Jordan and Wilt Chamberlain did better than his 27.4 points per game average. He was named to the NBA Silver Anniversary Team the same year he retired. Many fans still consider him to be the finest forward ever to play the game.

West said, "He had that wonderful, magical instinct for making plays and doing things that you had to just stop and watch. He is without a doubt one of the truly great people who played this game."[5]

ELGIN BAYLOR

BORN: September 16, 1934, Washington, D.C.

HIGH SCHOOL: Phelps Vocational High School, Spingarn High
School, Washington, D.C.

COLLEGE: The College of Idaho; University of Seattle.

PRO: Minneapolis Lakers, 1958–1960; Los Angeles Lakers, 1960–1972.

HONORS: #1 NBA Draft Pick, 1958; NBA Rookie of the Year, 1959;
Elected to Naismith Memorial Basketball Hall of Fame, 1976.

Baylor reaches up to block a shot. From 1959 to 1970, he played in
every NBA All-Star game except one. He was named co-MVP in the
1959 game.

LARRY BIRD

Larry Bird's determination and hard work helped bring the Boston Celtics to three NBA Championships in the 1980s, echoing their former glory of the 1960s.

THE HOUSTON ROCKETS WERE POISED to tie the 1986 NBA finals at three games all. Then Larry Bird got mad. He started screaming at his teammates, lunging on the court for loose balls and showing no mercy to the Rockets. By the end of the first half, he had 16 points, 8 assists, and 8 rebounds, and Boston led, 55–38. "I didn't want this day to slip away from me," he said.[1] It didn't. Boston won, 114–97.

By then Bird had a reputation as an incredible competitor. "Look in his eyes," said Dominique Wilkins, "and you see a killer."[2] On the court, Larry seemed invincible. After the victory over Houston, Larry said, "I just felt there was no one in the league who could stop me if I was playing hard."[3]

Nobody played harder than Bird. "The number one thing is desire," he said. "The ability to do the things you have to do to become a basketball player. I don't think you can teach anyone desire. I think it's a gift. I don't know why I have it, but I do."[4]

In a playoff game with the Pistons in 1987, Bird went up for the winning shot. But it was blocked beautifully by Dennis Rodman. Detroit had the ball and a 1-point lead, and Larry had been knocked to the floor. Isiah Thomas was going to run out the clock by flipping a soft easy pass to Bill Laimbeer. But by then Bird had jumped up and he intercepted the ball. Out of the corner of his eye, he saw teammate Dennis Johnson racing for the basket. Larry heaved the ball to Johnson, who laid it up for the winning shot.

Bird had been working on his basketball skills ever since he was a kid in French Lick, Indiana. At first, he practiced by tossing a rubber ball into a coffee can. By the time he was in high school, he was a six-foot nine-inch star, and he was dunking a real ball in a real net.

In the finals of the Missouri Valley tournament in his senior year with Indiana State University, Bird broke his left thumb midway through the game. That didn't stop him. The trainer taped it up and Bird was back out on the court. Indiana State won that one, part of a thirty-three-game winning streak.

Bird loved pressure. Time was running out in the seventh game of the 1981 playoffs against the Philadelphia 76ers. He made two steals and blocked Julius Erving's layup. Then he took a rebound, dribbled the length of the court, and sunk the winning basket. "I wanted the ball in my hands for the last shot," he said, "not in anybody else's hands in the world."[5]

In the 1980s, Bird and Magic Johnson of the Los Angeles Lakers were the game's most popular players. They were both big men who moved with speed and grace. Their teams met in the 1984 NBA finals. The fifth game was played in Boston Garden, an arena without air conditioning. While Magic and the other Lakers wilted in the 97-degree heat, Larry was as hot as the weather. He scored 34 points, and Boston won, 121–103. He averaged 27 points and 14 rebounds per game in the series, which the Celtics won, four games to three.

"With Larry, basketball is his life," Magic said. "He has great heart and guts. . . . Of all the people I play against, the only one I truly fear—or worry about—is Larry Bird."[6]

Bird won three straight MVP awards (1984, 1985, 1986). He and the Celtics appeared in the NBA finals five times, winning three titles. He retired after helping the U.S. Dream Team win the 1992 Olympic gold medal.

Bob Cousy, the great Celtics guard, said, "Larry Bird came along with all the skills, all the things a basketball player has to do. I think he's the greatest."[7]

LARRY BIRD

BORN: December 7, 1956, West Baden, Indiana.

HIGH SCHOOL: Springs Valley High School, French Lick, Indiana.

COLLEGE: University of Indiana, Indiana State University.

PRO: Boston Celtics, 1979–1992.

HONORS: NBA Rookie of the Year, 1980; NBA MVP, 1984–1986.

Larry Bird was known as the three-point king. When he retired in 1992, he had made more three-point field goals than any other player in NBA history.

WILT CHAMBERLAIN

NOBODY ELSE IN PROFESSIONAL BASKETBALL ever had a day like the one Wilt Chamberlain had on March 2, 1962.

His Philadelphia Warriors' teammates kept feeding him the ball, and he kept dropping it through the hoop. In the first period, he had 23 of the Warriors' 41 points. By halftime, his total was 41. After 28 in the third quarter, Wilt had 69, just 9 short of the record he had set earlier in the season.

It only took four more minutes for him to hit 79—and he was still shooting. The only way the New York Knicks could stop him was to foul him. Then he just made the free throws.

With less than a minute to go, he had 98 points. Then he went up to grab a soft pass and stuff it through the hoop. He had 100 points! Philadelphia had won, 169–141, but nobody really cared. Everybody was talking about Wilt's incredible performance. He had made 36 of 63 shots from the floor and dropped in 28 of 32 free throw tries.

When he was a six-foot eleven-inch ninth grader, Chamberlain's Overbrook High School team played for the Philadelphia city championship. He tried to stay under the basket where his height would allow him to get lots of easy points. But West Catholic foiled that strategy by surrounding him with four players. Wilt couldn't get the ball, and his team lost.

Throughout his college and early pro career, that was the way it went. Chamberlain wanted to be in close to the net for easy dunks and short shots off the backboard. If his opponents could keep him from getting the ball or block the lane so that he couldn't move in, he was frustrated and his team usually lost. But if he got the ball and got under the basket, he was unstoppable.

WILT CHAMBERLAIN

Chamberlain ended his career at the University of Kansas with a scoring average of 29.9. Then he played with the Harlem Globetrotters for a year before joining the Philadelphia Warriors.

In 1957, Chamberlain was the most valuable player in the National Collegiate Athletic Association tournament. But his team, the University of Kansas, lost the final game, 54–53, in triple overtime. He left college when he was a senior to play a year with the Harlem Globetrotters.

In his rookie season with the Warriors (1959–1960), Wilt led the league in scoring (37.6 points per game) and rebounding (27 per game). But Philadelphia was knocked out of the playoffs by Bill Russell and the Boston Celtics. Chamberlain was so angry that he said he was quitting basketball. Many fans said they wouldn't miss him. They said he was a ball hog who couldn't win big games. Others thought he was just a big bully with no skills who was only good because he was seven feet one inch tall.

Of course, Wilt changed his mind and didn't retire. He played thirteen more seasons in the NBA. He filled arenas across the country, but almost everybody wanted to see his team lose. "I guess most fans are for the little man and the underdog, and Wilt is neither," said Franklin Mieuli, former owner of the Warriors.[1]

Throughout most of his career, Chamberlain's dreams of an NBA championship continued to be thwarted by Russell and the Celtics. But in 1967, Wilt finally led the Philadelphia 76ers to the title. Five years later, as a member of the Los Angeles Lakers, he won his second championship and was named the finals MVP.

Chamberlain is remembered as one of the biggest, strongest men ever to play the game. When he took a rebound, it sounded like gunfire because he slapped the ball so hard. Bob Lanier, a six-foot ten-inch giant, said Chamberlain was so strong he "lifted me up and moved me like a coffee cup so he could get position."[2]

WILT CHAMBERLAIN

BORN: August 21, 1936, Philadelphia, Pennsylvania.

High SCHOOL: Overbrook, Philadelphia, Pennsylvania.

COLLEGE: University of Kansas.

PRO: Philadelphia Warriors, 1959–1962; San Francisco Warriors, 1962–1965; Philadelphia 76ers, 1965–1968; Los Angeles Lakers, 1968–1973.

RECORDS: Most career rebounds, 23,924; Highest rebounds per game average, 22.9.

HONORS: NBA Rookie of the Year, 1960; NBA MVP, 1960, 1966–1968; Elected to Naismith Memorial Basketball Hall of Fame, 1978.

Two of the greatest NBA stars of the early 1970s, Chamberlain and Kareem Abdul-Jabbar battle it out on the court.

JULIUS ERVING

Dr. J. was so popular, he was elected to every All-Star Game from 1977 to 1987. Twice, in 1977 and 1983, he was named All-Star Game MVP.

JULIUS ERVING

MOSES MALONE AND JULIUS ERVING powered the Philadelphia 76ers into the 1983 NBA finals against Kareem Abdul-Jabbar, Magic Johnson, and the Los Angeles Lakers. The 76ers won the first three games, but trailed late in the fourth game, 106–104.

During a time-out, Erving let his team know that he was not about to lose. They had made it to the finals twice before, only to be beaten by the Lakers. "I'm taking over," Julius told his teammates.[1] That's just what he did. Right away he stole the ball and raced downcourt for a dunk that tied the game. Then he sank a basket and a free throw. Finally he went over Magic with a one-handed basket. The 76ers won easily, 115–108.

Erving grew up in Hempstead, New York. When he was still in high school, he met Abdul-Jabbar. "I remember this skinny, bony kid," Kareem said. "We measured hands once. His were bigger. He played one-handed and stuffed over everybody."[2] It was about that time that he picked up the nickname "The Doctor."

Erving played well enough at Roosevelt High School to be recruited by more than a hundred colleges. He chose the University of Massachusetts. There he averaged 27 points and 19 rebounds a game as a junior. Instead of staying at school for his senior year, Dr. J. joined the Virginia Squires in the new American Basketball Association (ABA).

At first the new league was best known for its red, white, and blue ball. But Dr. J. quickly attracted attention with his graceful, exciting moves on the court. He could block shots, pass, and dunk like nobody else. One-on-one there was no one in the ABA who could stop him. He seemed to be able to hang in the air over their heads. How did he do it? "Sometimes on a straight rise," he joked, "you sort of put your air brake on and wait for the defense to go down."[3] Children on playgrounds all over America copied his moves. One of them was a skinny kid in North Carolina named Michael Jordan.

Playing with the New York Nets, Dr. J. had 45 points against the Denver Nuggets in the first game of the 1976 ABA finals. His last basket, a jumper at the buzzer, clinched a 120–118 win. Two games later, he had 8 straight points in the last minute and a half as the Nets won, 117–111. Soon after New York took the championship, four games to two, the ABA folded. Erving then finished up his career with the Philadelphia 76ers in the NBA.

The new team and new league didn't change his style at all. The Doctor was still one of the most popular and respected players in the game. Off the court he was known as an intelligent, eloquent spokesman for basketball. In a poll of sports reporters, he was named "the nicest guy in sports."

"I've always tried to tell myself that the work itself is the thing, that win, lose, or draw, the work is really what counts," Erving said. "Every game, every night, I did the best I could."[4]

In the 1970s, he was the most popular player in the NBA. Fans loved to watch his dunks and the incredible moves he made on the court. "Sometimes I watch Julius do something that I know I'll never see again on a basketball floor," said his teammate Brian Taylor. "He's a legend in his own time."[5]

JULIUS ERVING

BORN: February 22, 1950, Roosevelt, New York.

HIGH SCHOOL: Roosevelt High School, Roosevelt, New York.

COLLEGE: University of Massachusetts.

PRO: Virginia Squires (ABA), 1971–1973; New York Nets (ABA), 1973–1976; Philadelphia 76ers, 1976–1987.

HONORS: NBA MVP, 1981; Elected to Naismith Memorial Basketball Hall of Fame, 1993.

No one in the NBA could hang in the air quite like Julius Erving. His excellent basketball skills and friendly personality off court helped make him one of the most popular players in the country.

MICHAEL JORDAN

SEVENTEEN SECONDS LEFT. DOWN BY one, 62–61, the University of North Carolina was running out of time in the 1982 NCAA championship game against Georgetown University. Then the ball got into the hands of freshman Michael Jordan. He calmly went up with a seventeen-foot jump shot. Swish! The Tar Heels were champions!

Michael had grown up in Wilmington, North Carolina. Most of his time was spent on his backyard court with his older brother Larry. Usually Larry won—until his little brother grew four inches the summer after his sophomore year in high school. After that Michael was just about unstoppable.

As a member of the Chicago Bulls in the NBA, he seemed to fly up to the basket. With the Bulls trailing, 100–99, against the Cleveland Cavaliers in the 1989 playoffs, Michael went up for a jump shot. But Craig Ehlo went up with him. Jordan waited until Ehlo had sailed past, then released the ball. It swished the net as the buzzer sounded.

How did he hang in the air while everybody else was coming back down? Jordan joked, "I spread my legs pretty wide in the air. Maybe they're just like wings, and they hold me up there a little bit."[1]

After three years and 1,788 points at North Carolina, Michael joined the Bulls. Just as he had copied Julius Erving, youngsters across the country now tried to copy his beautiful, graceful dunks—and his trademark hanging-out tongue.

In the 1986 playoffs, he scored 63 points against the Boston Celtics. Nobody, not even Wilt Chamberlain, had ever gotten that many points in a playoff game. The next year, he

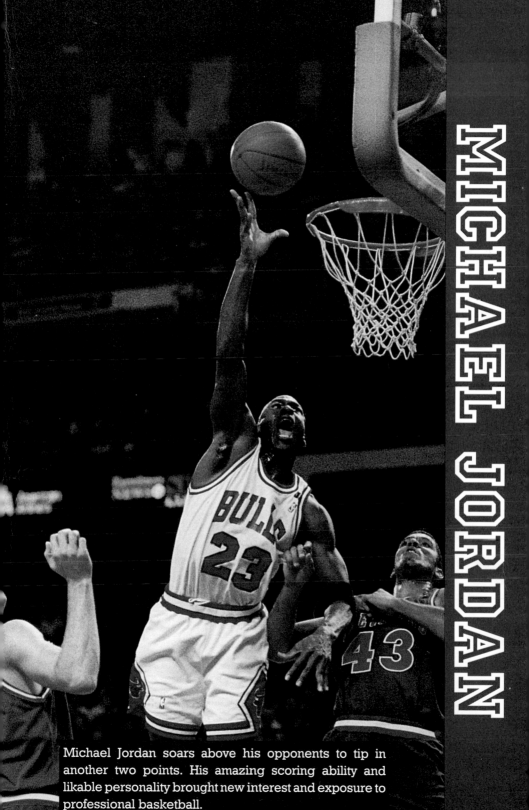

MICHAEL JORDAN

Michael Jordan soars above his opponents to tip in another two points. His amazing scoring ability and likable personality brought new interest and exposure to professional basketball.

hit 26 fourth-quarter points, including a last-second game-tying jump shot against the Detroit Pistons. After an overtime period, the Bulls had a 125–120 win and Michael had 61 points. He took his first NBA scoring title that season with 3,041 points, the first player to get that many since Chamberlain. He was soon the dominant athlete in the league. Chuck Daly, then the coach of the Detroit Pistons, said, "Jordan is a one-man wrecking crew."[2]

In 1991, Jordan led the Bulls past Magic Johnson and the Los Angeles Lakers in the NBA finals. He cried with joy as he held the championship trophy. The next season he danced on the scorer's table after the Bulls beat the Portland Trail Blazers for their second championship. Then in 1993, the Bulls made it three in a row by defeating the Phoenix Suns.

Jordan retired in 1993 after seven consecutive scoring titles. By then he was the most popular and highest-paid athlete in the world. He had earned the respect of the fans who watched him and the players who competed against him.

"No one was ever better than him," said Larry Bird. "He was a true joy to watch on the court whether he was your opponent or your teammate."[3] Shaquille O'Neal said, "One day when I have a son, I'm going to be able to say I played with Jordan."[4]

After retiring from basketball, Michael surprised almost everybody by signing a minor league baseball contract. "I chose to try to play baseball just to see if I could," he said. "It's one of the wishes my father had and I had as a kid." Many people doubted if he would be good enough to make it to the major leagues. But Jordan said, "I've never been afraid to fail . . . I think I'm strong enough as a person to accept failure. But I can't accept not trying."[5]

MICHAEL JORDAN

BORN: February 17, 1963, Brooklyn, New York.

HIGH SCHOOL: Emsley A. Laney, Wilmington, North Carolina.

COLLEGE: University of North Carolina.

PRO: Chicago Bulls, 1984–1993.

RECORDS: Highest career scoring average, 32.3; Shares record for most seasons leading league in scoring, 7.

HONORS: NBA Rookie of the Year, 1985; NBA MVP, 1988, 1991, 1992.

Even Michael Jordan's teammates were amazed by his aerial acrobatics. Using his ability to hang in the air, Jordan stuffed in an all-time record 32.3 points per game career average.

KARL MALONE

Karl "The Mailman" Malone shares the single-game playoff record for most free throws in one half, 19. He tied the record in a 1991 playoff game against the Portland Trail Blazers.

KARL MALONE

WHEN JOHN STOCKTON GETS THE ball, Karl Malone heads for the basket, and the Utah Jazz's opponents are in trouble. Stockton's job is to get the ball to his teammate, and then it's Malone's turn to deliver. That's why the fans call him "The Mailman."

Every season, Malone averages around 30 points a game and the Jazz win around 50 games. Malone and Stockton were both members of the 1992 U.S. Olympic squad, the Dream Team, that buried the competition in Barcelona, Spain. Karl averaged 13 points per game, third best on the team.

When he was a young boy, he didn't give much thought to basketball. Instead he told his mother, "Mama, I'm going to own me a big truck someday."[1] After signing a big contract with the Jazz, he finally achieved his goal. He now owns a huge semitrailer truck that sits in his garage in Salt Lake City. During the off-season he makes deliveries with the rig, signing autographs at each stop. When he retires from basketball, he plans to have a fleet of trucks and call his company "Malone Enterprises."

The Mailman earned his nickname starring for Louisiana Tech. But it wasn't until the 1986–1987 season that he became a power in the NBA. That year he averaged 21.7 points per game. For three seasons he was second in scoring to Michael Jordan. Among active players, only Dominique Wilkins has a better career-scoring average.

Karl has earned regular appearances in the NBA All-Star games. In 1989, he scored 28 points and grabbed 9 rebounds to lead the West to victory. That earned him MVP honors.

Malone is proud of his reputation as one of the toughest men in the NBA. He's big and strong and isn't afraid to throw his weight around on the court. Of course, it's kind of hard to push around a guy who's six feet nine inches tall. Karl is also known for his temper. He's usually one of the league leaders in technical fouls.

During the off-season when he's not driving his truck, Malone works hard to stay in shape. He exercises daily in his own weight room. He even taped an eight-part series on bodybuilding—"Karl Malone's Muscle Minute"—for the NBA TV show "Inside Stuff."

Jazz coach Jerry Sloan knows how hard The Mailman has worked to become an NBA star: "He's 100 percent better than when he started. . . . He has always done the things he needed [to do] to become better."[2] Larry Bird was also impressed. "Karl Malone is another awesome player. He just gets it, puts his head down and goes."[3]

Ever since he began playing basketball, Karl has looked at the game as a challenge. He enjoys getting in his opponents' faces, and he likes trying to prove he's better than the players he's going against. "In this business, everyone always says what you can't do," he said. "Guys say you can't shoot from outside so you start shooting from the outside and making them. Then it's that you can't play defense so you start playing defense. You throw it back at those same critics."[4]

Malone compares playing basketball to driving his big rig in the off-season. "You know what I feel like when I'm driving?" he asks. "A runaway truck under control. I guess that's kind of what I'm like on the basketball court, huh?"[5]

KARL MALONE

BORN: July 24, 1963, Summerfield, Louisiana.

HIGH SCHOOL: Summerfield High School, Summerfield, Louisiana.

COLLEGE: Louisiana Tech University.

PRO: Utah Jazz, 1985– .

Malone has helped bring the Utah Jazz up from the bottom of the league to the top of the Midwest Division.

Oscar Robertson

Even In High School, It was easy to tell Oscar Robertson was somebody special. Whenever the Crispus Attucks Tigers were leading in the closing minutes of play, "The Big O" put on a one-man show, racing around the court, dribbling as time ran out. The cheers grew louder and louder. Finally, just before the buzzer, Oscar would put up a game-ending shot. Usually it went in. The fans loved it.

But Robertson was more than just a showboat. He was a fine athlete who led Attucks to a pair of Indiana State championships. He also set an Indianapolis record with a high jump of six feet two and one-eighth inches.

The Robertsons lived in a poor, dangerous neighborhood in Indianapolis. "People were doing all kinds of wrong things," said Mrs. Robinson, "and I had to tell my children why they had to be different."[1] She made sure her kids stayed out of trouble by keeping busy with schoolwork and sports. Bailey, the oldest, later played for the Harlem Globetrotters. After graduating from high school, Oscar attended the University of Cincinnati.

In college, The Big O was tough—and he knew how to score. "If Oscar were a fighter, he could make a million," said Cincinnati coach George Smith.[2] In his first year, he averaged 35.1 points per game. Against North Texas State in 1960, he scored 62 points. He was a three-time All-American.

But there was much more to Robertson's game than just scoring. He was an all-around player who was also a superb rebounder and passer. He was always popular with fans who appreciated his hustle and his skills.

When he scored 2,165 points in 1960–1961 for the

OSCAR ROBERTSON

Oscar Robertson scored 2,165 points during his first season in the NBA, and he was named Rookie of the Year for 1960–1961.

Cincinnati Royals, he was named NBA Rookie of the Year. Three years later he was the league MVP. While he was with the Royals, he led the league six times in assists and usually averaged at least 30 points a game.

Oscar had ten great seasons with the Royals, but he rarely got a chance to "show off his stuff" in the postseason. Cincinnati never took an NBA championship. But Robertson almost always turned in great performances in the league's All-Star games. Three times he was named All-Star Most Valuable Player.

In 1971, he was elected to the NBA's Silver Anniversary Team. Only Wilt Chamberlain got more votes. But by then, Oscar was no longer in Cincinnati. The year before, he had been traded to the Milwaukee Bucks. He told his new teammates, " The only thing that matters in this game is being No. 1."[3] One of his teammates in Milwaukee was superstar center Lew Alcindor (later to be known as Kareem Abdul-Jabbar). For the good of the team, Robertson changed his style of play. Instead of scoring himself, he got the ball to Alcindor, who led the NBA with a 31.7 average in 1970–1971. The Bucks had a 66-16 regular season before dropping the Baltimore Bullets four games to none in the finals. Robertson celebrated the 118–106 victory in the last game by scoring 30 points of his own.

When Oscar retired in 1974, he was second to Wilt Chamberlain in career points scored. Magic Johnson is the only player who has had more assists.

"Oscar is not as fast as some ballplayers," Wilt Chamberlain said, "and not as good a shooter as others, but he knows how to put everything together better than anyone else."[4]

Oscar Robertson

BORN: November 24, 1938, Charlotte, Tennessee.

HIGH SCHOOL: Crispus Attucks High School, Indianapolis, Indiana.

COLLEGE: University of Cincinnati.

PRO: Cincinnati Royals, 1960–1970; Milwaukee Bucks, 1970–1974.

HONORS: NBA Rookie of the Year, 1961; NBA MVP, 1964; Elected to Naismith Memorial Basketball Hall of Fame, 1979.

"The Big O" was an all-around player, not just a scoring machine. He led the NBA in assists for six seasons: 1961, 1962, 1964, 1965, 1966, and 1969.

JERRY WEST

EARLY IN THE **1959 NCAA** tournament, the West Virginia Mountaineers trailed St. Joseph, 67–49. Then Jerry West went wild. He got 21 points in the next nine minutes, leading the way to a 95–92 victory.

In the third game of the 1962 NBA finals, Jerry's 4 straight points for the Los Angeles Lakers tied the game, 115–115, with four seconds left. Sam Jones tried to throw the ball inbounds to Bob Cousy, but Jerry stole it and took off for the other end of the court. Time was running out. The Laker fans screamed for him to shoot the ball. But West kept dribbling. Finally he laid the ball in just as the buzzer sounded. "I had deflected the ball on the run," he said calmly. "I knew I would have enough time."[1]

Then in game three of the 1970 finals, the Lakers were down, 102–100, with three seconds to go. Wilt Chamberlain passed the ball to West, who dribbled three times at mid-court, then released a sixty-foot desperation shot. It was good and the game was tied!

That's why they called Jerry West "Mr. Clutch." When his team needed the basket, the other players always seemed to make sure he got the ball.

Jerry grew up with five brothers and sisters in Cabin Creek, West Virginia, a tiny mining town. He broke his ankle during his sophomore year on the East Bank High School basketball team. He had to practice hard for many weeks to get back in shape. Before he graduated, he had the school record for points scored.

In his years with the Lakers, West broke his nose nine times. Those injuries didn't even slow him down. The trainers

JERRY WEST

Jerry West joined the Lakers for their first season playing in Los Angeles. He spent his entire career there and in 1966 set the NBA record for most free throws made in a season, 840.

would wrap his nose up with white tape and he played anyway. During the 1969 finals he pulled a hamstring muscle, but he played the last two games anyway, wearing a heavy bandage. Despite that injury, he earned MVP honors.

West's team finally won the NBA championship in 1972 when the Lakers whipped the New York Knicks four games to one. "I played terrible basketball in the finals and we won," he said. "I had contributed so much in other years when we lost. . . . I was playing so poorly that the team overcame me. Maybe that's what a team is all about.[2]

Jerry was only the fifth NBA player to score 20,000 points. When he retired in 1974, he had 25,192. His 27-points-per-game average is still fourth best in league history. Fans still talk about the game in which he scored 63 against the Knicks.

Have you ever seen the NBA logo with a silhouette of a player dribbling the ball? West was the model for the player. That's the way millions of fans remember him—charging down the court for the basket. Red Auerbach, the legendary Celtics coach, said, "When you begin talking about the all-around great players of basketball, a pretty good starting point is Jerry West."[3]

But today Jerry is remembered for more than just his skill at the game he loved. As Bill Russell, Boston's superstar center, told him, "The greatest honor a man can have is the respect and friendship of his peers. You have that more than any man I know."[4]

BORN: May 28, 1938, Cheylan, West Virginia.

HIGH SCHOOL: East Bank High School, East Bank, West Virginia.

COLLEGE: University of West Virginia.

PRO: Los Angeles Lakers, 1960–1973.

RECORDS: Most free throws made in a season (1960), 840.

HONORS: Elected to Naismith Memorial Basketball Hall of Fame, 1979.

Jerry West was named the Most Valuable Player of the 1969 NBA Finals, even though the Lakers lost to the Celtics. He is the only player for a losing team to ever receive the award.

DOMINIQUE WILKINS

Wilkins holds the NBA single-game record for most free throws without a miss, 23. The record was sweet revenge, as it came in a game against his chief rival, Michael Jordan of the Chicago Bulls.

DOMINIQUE WILKINS

EARLY IN HIS CAREER, DOMINIQUE Wilkins was criticized as a showoff who was more interested in making fancy dunks than in helping his team to win. Some of his teammates said he was only on the court for himself. They even complained about the way he warmed up. Because he worked so hard on his pregame dunks, they said he was tired by the time the game began.

Dominique listened to the criticism and decided to change his style of play. He began trying jump shots and working out plays with his teammates.

The new strategy worked. He still scored a lot of points, but now his Atlanta Hawks were winning. In the 1985–1986 season, he was the league's leading scorer, with 2,366 points (30.3 per game). That year the Hawks made the playoffs. In the first game against Detroit, he never dunked the ball, but he did score 50 points. Atlanta dusted off Detroit three games to one.

Wilkins was pleased that as he gained experience, he was becoming a smarter, better player. "If people learned to respect the way I played, they must understand that maturity had much to do with it," he said. "I really didn't change much of my overall game. I just paid more attention to all the individual parts."[1]

When 'Nique was a teenager growing up in Washington, North Carolina, he regularly gave his mother money to buy groceries. "I always thought he was doing odd jobs, raking grass," Mrs. Wilkins said.[2] More than a few times she was even afraid Dominique had stolen the money. But her son had earned it playing basketball. He'd compete one on one against other men for a dollar a game. He almost always won.

It was in high school that Wilkins first became known for his flashy dunks that would later earn him the nickname "The Human Highlight Film." At the University of Georgia, he would score 732 points as a sophomore.

After Wilkins left college, he was drafted by the Utah Jazz. But the Hawks desperately wanted him to play in Atlanta. They gave the Jazz two players and a million dollars for 'Nique. Soon he was one of the most popular athletes in Atlanta.

Early in his pro career, Dominique proved he could score. He had 2,217 points in the 1984–1985 season, then led the league the next season. For the two years after that, only Chicago's Michael Jordan had more points.

Even though his scoring average fell, the 1990–1991 season was one of Wilkins's best. Because he was concentrating on helping his team, he had more assists and rebounds than ever. Early the next year he had 52 points in a game against the New York Knicks. But after tearing his Achilles tendon, he missed the last thirty-eight games of the season.

By 1993, 'Nique had more points than any other player in Hawks history—and he was still piling up big numbers. His coach Bob Weiss said Wilkins had learned to be a real team player. "He wants to . . . be recognized as a complete player, and not just a super talent. And he's done that in a lot of ways, like breaking his habit of leaking out to get on the fast break. He stayed to battle on the boards and that gave him more rebounds."[3]

But then Dominique was traded from Atlanta to the Los Angeles Clippers on February 24, 1994. He may have switched teams, but he still had the same goal. Before he retired, Michael Jordan had complained that Wilkins was trying to take away his scoring title. "No, I'm not," was 'Nique's instant reply. "It's your NBA title that I want."[4]

DOMINIQUE WILKINS

BORN: January 12, 1960, Paris, France.

HIGH SCHOOL: Washington High School, Washington, North Carolina.

COLLEGE: University of Georgia.

PRO: Atlanta Hawks, 1982–1994; Los Angeles Clippers, 1994– .

RECORD: Most free throws in a game without a miss, 23.

Dominique Wilkins has been one of the premier scorers in the NBA. In 1986 he lead the league in scoring.

NOTES BY CHAPTER

Kareem Abdul-Jabbar

1. Larry Bird and Bob Ryan, *Drive: The Story of My Life* (New York: Bantam Books, 1989), pp. 272–273.
2. Earvin "Magic" Johnson, Jr., and Roy S. Johnson, *Magic's Touch* (New York: Addison-Wesley Publishing Company, 1989), p. 170.
3. Art Berke (editor-in-chief), *The Lincoln Library of Sports Champions*, vol. 1 (Columbus, Ohio: Frontier Press Company, 1985), pp. 30-31.
4. Editors, Salem Press, *Great Athletes*, vol. 1 (Pasadena, Calif.: Salem Press, 1992), p. 7.

Elgin Baylor

1. Roland Lazenby, *The NBA Finals* (Dallas: Taylor Publishing Company, 1990), p. 87.
2. Bill Gutman, *The Pictorial History of Basketball* (New York: Gallery Books, 1988), p. 72.
3. Alexander Wolff, *100 Years of Hoops* (Birmingham, Ala.: Oxmoor House, 1988), p. 118.
4. Ibid.
5. Lazenby, p. 88.

Larry Bird

1. Roland Lazenby, *The NBA Finals* (Dallas: Taylor Publishing Company, 1990), pp. 230–231.
2. Alexander Wolff, *100 Years of Hoops* (Birmingham, Ala.: Oxmoor House, 1988), p. 120.
3. Billy Packer and Roland Lazenby, *The Golden Game* (Dallas: Taylor Publishing Company, 1991), p. 199.
4. Lazenby, p. 213.
5. Art Berke (editor-in-chief), *The Lincoln Library of Sports Champions*, vol. 2 (Columbus, Ohio: Frontier Press Company, 1985), p. 82.
6. Magic Johnson, "Foreword," from Larry Bird and Bob Ryan, *Drive: The Story of My Life* (New York: Bantam Books, 1989), p. xi.
7. Wolff, p. 120.

Wilt Chamberlain

1. Roland Lazenby, *The NBA Finals* (Dallas: Taylor Publishing Company, 1990), pp. 109–110.
2. Alexander Wolff, *100 Years of Hoops* (Birmingham, Ala.: Oxmoor House, 1988), p. 122.

Julius Erving

1. Roland Lazenby, *The NBA Finals* (Dallas: Taylor Publishing Company, 1990), p. 212.
2. Art Berke (editor-in-chief), *The Lincoln Library of Sports Champions*, vol. 5 (Columbus, Ohio: Frontier Press Company, 1985), p. 82.
3. Alexander Wolff, *100 Years of Hoops* (Birmingham, Ala.: Oxmoor House, 1988), p. 72.

4. Lazenby, p. 212.

5. Berke, p. 86.

Michael Jordan

1. Alexander Wolff, *100 Years of Hoops* (Birmingham, Ala.: Oxmoor House, 1988), p. 72.

2. Chuck Daly, with Joe Falls, *Daly Life* (Grand Rapids, Mich.: Masters Press, 1990), p. 228.

3. "What Michael Means to Us," *Newsweek* (October/November, 1993), p. 45.

4. Ibid., p. 43.

5. Associated Press Dispatch (February 8, 1994).

Karl Malone

1. J. McCallum, "Big Wheel," *Sports Illustrated* (April 27, 1992), p. 66.

2. Jack Clary, *The NBA: Today's Stars, Tomorrow's Legends* (Rocky Hill, Conn.: Great Pond Publishing, 1992), pp. 60–63.

3. Larry Bird and Bob Ryan, *Drive: The Story of My Life* (New York: Bantam Books, 1989), p. 271.

4. Clary, p. 60.

5. McCallum, pp. 69-70.

Oscar Robertson

1. Art Berke (editor-in-chief), *The Lincoln Library of Sports Champions*, vol. 15 (Columbus, Ohio: Frontier Press Company, 1985), p. 64.

2. Alexander Wolff, *100 Years of Hoops* (Birmingham, Ala.: Oxmoor House, 1988), p. 136.

3. Ibid.

4. Bill Gutman, *The Pictorial History of Basketball* (New York: Gallery Books, 1988), p. 72.

Jerry West

1. Roland Lazenby, *The NBA Finals* (Dallas: Taylor Publishing Company, 1990), p. 87.

2. Lazenby, p. 139.

3. Art Berke (editor-in-chief), *The Lincoln Library of Sports Champions*, vol. 19 (Columbus, Ohio: Frontier Press Company, 1985), p. 8.

4. Alexander Wolff, *100 Years of Hoops* (Birmingham, Ala.: Oxmoor House, 1988), p. 140.

Dominique Wilkins

1. Jack Clary, *The NBA: Today's Stars, Tomorrow's Legends* (Rocky Hill, Conn.: Great Pond Publishing, 1992), p. 104.

2. Editors, Salem Press, *Great Athletes*, vol. 19 (Pasadena, Calif.: Salem Press, 1992), p. 2759.

3. Ibid., p. 104.

4. Ibid.

INDEX